<u>Contents</u>

|   | *Foreword to new edition* | p. 4 |
|---|---|---|
|   | *Introduction* | p. 5 |
| 1 | *Food and drink* | p. 18 |
| 2 | *Sports and games* | p. 38 |
| 3 | *Songs and carols* | p. 46 |
| 4 | *Guising* | p. 59 |
| 5 | *Superstition* | p. 73 |
| 6 | *The end of the season* | p. 93 |
|   | *Bibliography* | p. 98 |

## Foreword to new edition

*Since publishing* The Auld Scots Yule *in 2019, I have done considerably more research into Scottish seasonal traditions, and have been able to add substantially more detail to every chapter, as well as identifying and correcting a few (thankfully minor!) errors.*

*The result is a book over 65% longer than the original, bursting with new and fascinating information. I hope that it will be enjoyed by anyone with an interest in this neglected area of Scotland's folkloric heritage.*

*Marcus Pitcaithly*

# THE AULD SCOTS YULE

*Christmas Traditions of Scotland*

*Expanded and Updated*

By Marcus Pitcaithly

MMXIX, MMXXV

To Chris and Steve

*The Auld Scots Yule* was first published by
Marcus Pitcaithly, July 2019
This expanded and updated edition first
published January 2025
© Marcus Pitcaithly 2019, 2025
ISBN (expanded edition): 978-1-917662-00-0

## Introduction

Famously, Hogmanay has historically been a bigger deal than Christmas in Scotland. Indeed, if there is an authentically Scottish Christmas tradition that has survived continuously outside the Northern Isles to the present day, it must be confined to Catholic corners of the Highlands. Christmas Day was not a public holiday in Scotland until 1958,[1] and most Scottish Protestants took little notice of it until around the same time. They then imported English and American traditions

---

[1] Nor was Boxing Day until 1974: Stewart, Gordon, https://soundcloud.com/you-better-run-records/tales-from-wyrd-scotland-episode-6-a-bleak-midwinter?in=you-better-run-records/sets/tales-from-wyrd-scotland. It did have some previous currency as "Sweetie Scone Day", when servants and tradesfolk would be given fruit scones in lieu of the boxed gifts more common in England; but as a general rule such distributions were saved for Handsel Monday.
(https://www.glasgowtimes.co.uk/news/18943087.boxing-day-scotland-celebrated-sweetie-scone-day/.)

wholesale; while Catholics of Irish and other immigrant stock preserved the customs of their ancestral lands.[2]

However, it had taken centuries for the Kirk to extinguish the festival completely. Certainly, it tried its hardest, backed from 1640 to 1712 by Parliamentary statute. But there was a long tradition of observance to overturn.[3]

Medieval Scottish kings had copied the practice of their English counterparts and used Christmas courts for political spectacle. William the Lion was crowned at Scone on Christmas Eve 1165; Alexander II, from his first Christmas court at Forfar in 1214, made a point of using the festival to settle disputes and make land grants. Notably, after finally wiping out the long rebellious MacWilliam family in 1230, he waited until Christmas to confer their

---

[2] My own father, born in 1949 to a Protestant Perthshire farmer and a Catholic Irish nurse, recalls my grandfather and the farm workers treating Christmas as an ordinary working day when he was a child.

[3] This observance is preserved in the family names Yuill and Zuil, which reportedly derive from ancestors born on Yule Day.

Earldom of Ross on his ally Farquhar MacTaggart in a ceremony at Elgin.

Perhaps the most noteworthy Christmas celebration attended by a King of Scots, however, happened in England. In 1251, the ten-year-old Alexander III travelled to York to be married to Margaret, daughter of England's Henry III. A whole street was set aside for his retinue to lodge in. He was knighted by Henry on Christmas Day, the English king using the ceremony as an occasion to try to wring an acknowledgement from Alexander of his suzerainty over Scotland. However, Alexander declared that he had not come to discuss such weighty matters of state, and would not do so without consulting his advisers.

A feast followed, provided by the Archbishop, at which sixty cows were devoured, the chronicler Matthew Paris denouncing the luxury and decadence of the celebrations; much drink having flowed, a brawl followed between the English and Scottish retinues, in which one man was killed and many others badly hurt. The wedding itself, scheduled for the morning of the 26th, was moved to before dawn, to avoid the crush of the crowds and the danger of further rioting. It may not sound like the most successful of Christmas parties, but it did help secure a generation of peace between the rival kingdoms, without the subjection Henry had hoped to impose.

A still more turbulent Yule was that kept by the Macnabs of Killin at some unspecified point in the Middle Ages. Legend has it that the Nishes, a family of marauders hiding out on an island in Loch Earn, attacked the caravan carrying the Laird of Macnab's Yule feast from Crieff to Killin, and carried it off to their watery fastness, feeling secure in the possession of the only boat on the loch; but the Macnab's sons carried a boat on their shoulders across the mountains from Loch Tay, and surprised the Nishes as they slept off their stolen repast, decapitating every man of them and taking the heads back to their father, as a grisly Christmas gift.[4]

The Reformation in 1560 did not lead immediately to suppression of the festival. In 1565, the burgesses and artificers of Aberdeen were required to make gifts of

---

[4] *The New Statistical Account of Scotland*, vol. 10 (Edinburgh, 1845), p. 580.

money to the town serjeants at Yule; and, of course, the Catholic Queen Mary celebrated the season. However, in 1567 Mary was forced to abdicate, and hardline Protestants gained complete control of the government. As early as 1573, the Session of St Andrews sentenced several persons to make satisfaction for "observing Yule Day". Yet in 1649 we find the same Session having to order it pronounced from every pulpit that "no Yule be keiped, but all be put to work" – to no avail, for in January 1650 many parishioners were arraigned and punished for celebrating the feast with games of "jollie at the goose".

Sadly, the details of this game are unknown. So too are those of the superstitious observances held on the Links of Aberdour the previous Yule, and the game "Lady Templeton", which was banned a few decades earlier by the Session of Ayr. Yet these proclamations are a good source of information on sixteenth and seventeenth century Yule customs. We might not know of Aberdeen's masked balls, or the popularity of Yule bread in Glasgow, without the Kirk's fulminations against them. (In the latter case, bakers were required to report on any attempt to purchase the prohibited loaves.)[5]

The relative power of different factions in early modern Scotland may indeed be judged by the status of the Yule Vacance, the holiday from duty taken by the Court of Session. Abolished after the Reformation, it was restored by James VI when he reached his majority, and reasserted by him in 1618; ceased again with the general repression of Yule in 1640; was restored again by Charles II; only to be abolished once more in 1690, and finally restored after the Union with England.[6] As late as 1743, however, the General

---

[5] Simpkins, John Ewart, *County Folk-Lore Vol. VII: Examples of Printed Folk-lore Concerning Fife with Some Notes on Clackmannan and Kinross-shires* (London, 1914), pp. 140-41; Rogers, Charles, *Social Life in Scotland from Early to Recent Times* (Edinburgh, 1884), Vol. II, pp. 205-06.

[6] *The Scots Weekly Magazine: A Repertory of Literary Entertainment. Original and Selected. November 1832 to April 1833* (Edinburgh, 1833), p. 50; Cobbett, William, *Cobbett's parliamentary history of England, from the Norman conquest, in 1066, to the year, 1803* (London, 36 v., 1810), Vol. VI, p. ccxxxviii.

Assembly of the Kirk was still denouncing the existence of this holiday as a national sin, as bad as the recent abolition of witch-burning. The most extreme Presbyterians condemned not only Yule, but the celebration of *any* feasts, and even the use of names instead of numbers for the twelve months and the days of the week.[7]

Despite this, in 1680, Yule celebrations were actually made the occasion of demonstrating Protestant zeal, when students in Edinburgh carried an effigy of the Pope up Blackfriars before exploding it with gunpowder. The original intent was to set light to the figure at the Abbey of Holyroodhouse, where the famously Catholic Duke of Albany, Lord High Commissioner of Scotland, was then residing. However, word of this plan reached the Duke, and four companies of soldiers (surely overkill!) were brought in to prevent it – only for the students to learn of this in turn, and alter their route to avoid

---

[7] Law, Robert, *Memorialls, or the Memorable Things that fell out within this Island of Brittain from 1638 to 1684*, ed. Sharpe, Charles Kirkpatrick (Edinburgh, 1818), p. 190.

the troops.[8] A few years later, when the Duke – now King James VII – was ousted by the Dutch invasion, December 1688 was marked by widespread protests against "Popish" Christmas services. A renewed ban would soon follow.

Many customs were indeed extinguished: but the celebration of the season persisted. As late as 1833, one Edinburgh magazine could date the decline of the Scots Yule to "within the last twenty or thirty years"[9], while another could note that labourers generally still refused to work on that day, and women to spin.[10] It seems that it was only with the general falling-off of the season's popularity across Britain around 1800 that the longstanding attempts at suppression at last succeeded, the famous English Christmas revival of the 1840s taking no hold in Scotland.[11] (In

---

[8] Ibid., pp. 174-75.

[9] *The Schoolmaster, and Edinburgh Weekly Magazine, Vols. 1-2* (Edinburgh, 1833), p. 385.

[10] *Scots Weekly Magazine 1832-33*, p. 51.

[11] It is notable, when one reads the famous *Statistical Accounts of Scotland*, that Christmas is much mentioned as a time of feast and idleness in the "old" accounts from the 1790s, far less so in the "new", put together from the mid 1830s

and published in 1845. Even so, as late as 1851, the Aberdeenshire poet William Anderson could write of "When Christmas cam roun' wi' its feastin' an' fun" (*Rhymes, Reveries, and Reminiscences* (Aberdeen, 1851)). Even in 1890, the Elgin storyteller Margaret Craig could still recount a version of the Cinderella story "Rashen-Coatie" in which the role of the royal ball in the famous French and German versions is played by the Yule Day kirk service, a glittering event which the nobility attend while their Yule dinner is prepared by servants at home: though this element of the story probably reflected the realities of a much earlier age. (*Folk-lore*, vol. 1 (1890), pp. 289-90.)

To some extent, the later nineteenth century did see some aping of the English Christmas among the upper classes, especially in Edinburgh and Glasgow: see *Folk-lore*, vol. 4 (1893), p. 310; also Henderson, William, *Notes on the folklore of the northern counties of England and the borders* (London, 1878), p. 64. There were also individual parishes where the Kirk was better disposed towards the season: at St Fergus in Aberdeenshire, the Session distributed flour to the poor every year on Yule Day, in accordance with the will of a benefactor who wished every family to have the opportunity to make their own cake. (*The New Statistical Account of Scotland*, vol. 12, p. 198.) A few similar bequests are found scattered around the Northern Isles, the festival persisted, complete with several days of unofficial holiday.)

But this meant that, when early Victorian folklorists began taking note of customs surrounding the seasons of the year, Yule was still a living memory in much of Scotland, having passed out of active celebration only a generation or so previously. The writings of these scholars are therefore a rich source of lore regarding how the season was celebrated in Scotland of old. And even if one popular rhyme could dismiss it as a miserable time compared to Easter:

"When Yule comes, dule comes,

---

other parishes. In Banff, the clergy were still more generous, taking up a Yule Een collection for the poor and specifically including non-Presbyterians among the distributees! (Sinclair, John, *The Statistical Account of Scotland 1791-99* (21v., Edinburgh, 1791-99), vol. 20 (1798), p. 336.

Catholics, of course, continued to celebrate the season as they always had: and Clyde Street Church in Glasgow, catering – in the days before large scale Irish immigration – mostly to Highland labourers, was opened "with great solemnity" for the Christmas Day mass in 1816.

> Cauld feet and legs;
> When Pasch comes, grace comes,
> Butter, milk, and eggs."[12]

- celebrated it clearly was, and with gusto. And of course, Hogmanay, which never went out of fashion, was part of the same season, and indeed shared many customs with Christmas Eve and Day. (So many, indeed, that some had most likely been simply transferred from the banned Catholic festival to the tolerated secular one.)

One thing that emerges quite clearly is that Christmas was very seldom called "Christmas" in any part of Scotland. The Gaelic name was *Nollaig*, derived from the Latin *Natalis* (shorthand for *Dies Natalis Christi*, "the day of Christ's birth"); and wherever Germanic tongues were spoken – Scots, English, or Norn – it was simply Yule or Yeel.

---

[12] Chambers, Robert, *Popular Rhymes of Scotland*, 3rd edition (Edinburgh and London, 1841), p. 388. This is all the more surprising given that Scotland has little trace of any native Easter traditions.

This comes from the Norse pagan feast commonly associated with the Winter Solstice, and whose celebration was kept up by medieval Orcadians and Shetlanders long after their conversion to Christianity. However, it is worth noting that the Solstice did not fall on the 21st December, its median date under the modern Gregorian Calendar. The old Julian Calendar's relation to the solar year drifted over time, so that by the time the United Kingdom adopted Gregorian dating in 1752 the median date of the Solstice had fallen back as far as 10th December; but most of medieval Europe had inherited the Roman tradition of observing it nominally on the 25th, which made conflation with Christmas natural. However, there is some evidence that the Norse Yule may originally have fallen as late as mid January [13] – which is perhaps why Shetlanders into the twentieth century extended Christmas celebrations for twenty-four days, and Up-Helly-Aa at the end of January remains the official end of

---

[13] Jarman, Cat, https://podfollow.com/gone-medieval/episode/698888ce9ff379c4196eb20d51c4613d75bbc169/view.

the season. Alternatively, this January Yule may even in pagan times have already been the *end* of a month-long Yule season beginning around the Solstice.

It was on Yule Night of 1154-55 that enemies of Erlend Haraldsson, a claimant to the earldom of Orkney, felt able to attack his house on Damsay, confident that he and his men – who kept the feast in the old style, Christians though they were – would be too drunk to resist: but whether this was the night of the astronomical solstice (14th December in the twelfth century), of the 24th – 25th, or of the conjectural January Yule, we cannot now know for sure. Whatever the date, they were successful, and Erlend was slain.[14]

---

[14] *Orkneyinga Saga*, chapters 92 – 104. The reference to a twelve day feast perhaps makes 24th December the most likely.

## 1: *Food and Drink*

> "Yule, Yule, Yule,
> Three puddings in a pule!
> Crack nuts and cry Yule!"[15]

Our earliest notice of the winter festivities in Scotland comes in Bishop Turgot's *Life of Saint Margaret, Queen of Scotland*, when he remarks on how the pious Queen[16] kept her Advent. Advent in medieval Christendom was a time of fasting before the Christmas revels, beginning from the fourth Sunday before Christmas Day (i.e. between 27th November and 3rd December, depending on when in the week the feast fell): but Turgot tells us that Margaret kept a second Lent in winter, fasting for a full forty days. Even Christmas itself she kept austerely, washing the feet of beggars with the

---

[15] Chambers, *Popular Rhymes*, p. 162. This celebratory exclamation had, by the 1840s, long outlived the actual consumption of puddings and nuts.

[16] English-born consort to Malcolm III, King of Scots 1058-93.

assistance of her husband, before he went about the business of state and she bewailed the wickedness of the world.

Lenten observance was highly politicised in the early Middle Ages, because of rival Christian sects' different ways of reckoning the date of Easter. Most Scots at the time favoured a method more akin to that of the Eastern Church than that of Rome, but according to Turgot their actual observance of the fast was lax by any standard: and Margaret was keen to enforce both Roman dating and strict observance. Advent, however, held no comparable meaning, and the Queen's forty days' fast was a private devotion in which her husband's subjects were not required to join.

The Advent fast may originally have arisen as a pointed difference from pagan observance in ancient Rome. It corresponded almost exactly to the Roman festivities of Brumalia and Saturnalia, and gave place to a fortnight's feasting just as the pagans would have been nursing their hangovers and heading back to work. But it had continued applications after the Roman era, giving people time to save enough luxurious comestibles for

Christmas and sharpening their appetites in time for its arrival. Be that as it may, the tradition that feasting began on the 25th long outlived the Reformation. To let a visitor go unfed on Yule Day was considered unspeakably bad luck.

In medieval Scotland, even monks feasted well when the Advent fast was over. The Abbot of Kelso was given by King Malcolm IV[17] the right to buy for a halfpenny one chicken from every house in the various vills belonging to the abbey, adding up to dozens of birds for the Christmas feast.[18] By the fifteenth century, however, the fast had become the occasion of those who could afford to hoarding corn, with a view to selling it at inflated prices: so that in 1449 an act was passed forbidding anyone to lay up greater stocks of corn than were necessary to feed their own families beyond Christmas Day, any surplus to be sent to market at the earliest opportunity.[19]

---

[17] Reigned 1153-65.

[18] Taylor, James, *The Pictorial History of Scotland, From The Roman Invasion to the Close of the Jacobite Rebellion. A.D. 79 – 1746, Vol. I* (London, 1859), p. 181.

[19] Ibid., p. 329.

Some areas did slightly anticipate the day itself. At Gleghornie, East Lothian, at least into the sixteenth century, a great crab hunt was held on the beach at the Solstice, sacks of crustaceans being brought back for a communal feast.[20] In Orkney's Mainland, the 17th of December was Sow Day, on which every family possessing pigs would slaughter one for the Yule feast, so that the meat might be hung for a week.[21] In northern Shetland, the last Sunday before Yule was called "Byanna's Sunday". The origins of the name are lost to time: but traditionally a boiled cow's head was eaten that day, the fat skimmed from the top of

---

[20] Crockett, Samuel Rutherford, *Raiderland: All about Grey Galloway, its stories, traditions, characters, and humours* (London, 1904), p. 96, citing the chronicler John Mair or Major. He reports that a similar tradition prevailed at the summer solstice.

[21] *Scots Weekly Magazine 1832-33*, p. 50. On Sanday, a "Yule sheep" slaughtered on Yule Een itself took the place of the pig. "And on the forenoon of that day," the *New Statistical Account* tells us, "there is a great gathering, at certain places, of all the men and sheep in the island, for the selection of the several victims." (*New Statistical Account*, vol. 15, p. 110.)

the pan and kept by, and the skull used to make a lamp, with candles in its eye sockets lit on Yule morning.[22]

The purpose of reserving the fat was to make *fat brose* or *Yule-brose* for the Yuletide breakfast, customary in many parts of the country. Elsewhere, the meat for this was boiled on Yule Een (Christmas Eve), traditionally given over to culinary preparations of all kinds. Fat brose was a sort of savoury porridge, made using animal fat (usually beef if it could be had) instead of water or milk. A breakfast of hot beef fat and oatmeal may sound unappetising, especially compared to the favoured Yule dinners of pork in the Orkneys and haggis in many parts of the Highlands. But for poor peasants in a cold country, it is easy to imagine that a rich hot meal would have been a very welcome start to a winter's day!

A correspondent to *Blackwood's Magazine* in 1821 described how a gold ring would be stirred into the communal pot, and the company hasten to gorge on the "half-boiling" brose: the one who found

---

[22] Towrie, Sigurd, orkneyjar.com/tradition/yule/yule6.htm.

the ring, according to superstition, would be the first to be married.[23] Until around the 1790s, at least one Lothian nobleman (his name now lost) is reported to have provided fat brose on Yule morning, followed by beef and ale, to all his tenantry and their families in the great hall.[24] This is reminiscent of the "bummacks" of seventeenth century Orkney, when feuers were expected to feast their tenants on Yule Day: though the latter custom had devolved in the eighteenth century to a dole of cakes given at the door.[25]

It was likely a Yule-brose that the unfortunate Maggy of Guildy was caught preparing, although the incident seems to

---

[23] *Scots Weekly Magazine 1832-33*, p. 52. Cf. the English custom of hiding a silver sixpence in a Christmas pudding.

[24] *Schoolmaster, Vol. 2*, p. 386.

[25] Urquhart, *Statistical Account*, vol. 15 (1795), pp. 393-94. When a Yule bummack was refused to one Jonet Rendall around 1628, she is said to have told the miserly gentleman that he should not see another Yule banquet – and indeed he died only fifteen days later, a fact material to Jonet's later conviction and execution for witchcraft. (Lynn, Elizabeth, *Witch Stories* (London, 1861), p. 71.)

have taken place later in the day than one might expect. Tradition relates that the Reverend James Goodsir, Minister of Monikie in Angus from 1717 to 1733, was in the habit of stalking about his parish on Christmas Day to make sure that none of his parishioners were indulging in illicit celebrations. One year, he was making such investigations in the village of Guildy, while old Maggy had a pan on the fire to boil off fat for the brose. Seeing the minister advancing across her kailyard:

> "She had just time to lift off the pot, but in her agitation could find no better place to hide it than below her bed-cover; this accomplished, she had got seated at her spinning-wheel by the time that his reverence entered, who paid her some compliments upon her conduct, contrasting it with that of some of her neighbours, who shewed less disposition to comply with the austerity of his injunctions. Maggy, in her solicitude to escape detection, overshot her own mark, for she echoed her

minister's remarks so zealously, that he felt a pleasure in prolonging his stay; but unfortunately for both, during the bitter censure of those who offered unrighteous sacrifice, or still 'longed for the flesh-pots of Egypt', Maggy's pot set fire to the bed-clothes, and the smoke came curling over the minister's shoulders. Maggy started up, flew to the bed, and, in her hurry to remove the clothes, overset the tell-tale pot, splashing Mr. Goodsir's legs with the hot and fat broth, &c. The consequence may easily be conjectured – Maggy's conduct was reported to the elder of the quarter, she became the laughing-stock of her neighbours, and had further to do public penance before the congregation, for the complicated crimes of heresy and hypocrisy."[26]

---

[26] Ibid., pp. 385-86. A minister in Elgin was similarly noted for patrolling his parish to

Perhaps more pleasant was the milk brose supped at Helya's Een (19th December) in the Shetlands.[27] But if there was a *less* appealing seasonal use of oats than fat brose, it was surely the making of sowans, a dish of fermented oat husks and meal. In Aberdeenshire, Yule-Een was known as Sowans Nicht from the traditional gathering of neighbours to enjoy this: no doubt it was made more palatable by being washed down with Yule ale, described as being made with hops, ginger, and treacle – far more Christmassy than fermented oat husks to modern

---

confiscate roast geese: MacDonald, Annie, and Johnstone, Jenny,
https://www.storiesofscotland.com/podcast/2021/12/21/bonus-christmas-crimes. Despite the cold weather, it was not unknown for people to take their work outdoors on Yule Day so that they could be *seen* to be labouring and not celebrating.

[27] Black, G. F. (collector), and Thomas, Northcote W. (editor), *County Folk-Lore Vol. III: Examples of Printed Folk-Lore concerning the Orkney and Shetland Islands* (London, 1903), p. 197.

tastes![28] A recipe for sowans can be found in F. Marian McNeill's *The Scots Kitchen*: in 2017, the food history blogger Catriona Sutherland assayed it, and took several attempts and considerable improvisation to produce something edible. (This may be because sowans were not always meant to be eaten. An article in the 1893 volume of the journal *Folk-lore* indicates that sowans were carried by young carollers as a symbol of the more nutritious fare they sought, and spattered on the doors of those who refused them admittance.[29])

In most areas, Yule Een was traditionally given over not to the supping of sowans, but to baking bannocks or "care-cakes", and boiling meat to make fat brose. The bannocks were of a cakey consistency, being made with eggs, though no recipe survives. A superstition existed in Angus that, if a Yule bannock fell apart in the baking, the baker would not live to see another Yule.[30] In parts of the North-East, it was customary to divide the

---

[28] Watson, William, *Glimpses o' Auld Lang Syne* (Aberdeen, 1905), p. 95.

[29] *Folk-lore*, v. 4 (1893), pp. 316-17.

[30] Chambers, *Popular Rhymes*, p. 163.

bannock among the family, each of whom would hide their piece until nightfall: for it to be found by someone else, or eaten before the sun set, would bring bad luck for the year ahead.[31]

In the Shetlands, oatcakes or ginger broonies called Yule-cakes took the place of the mainland care-cakes. One was made for each child in the family: they were round, with a hole in the centre, and pinched into points around the edges, in obvious solar symbolism.[32]

Even animals were treated to a festive breakfast. The last handful of corn gathered at the end of harvest, known as the "maiden", was preserved until Yule (or until the New Year in some areas), either to be added to the general food-trough or to be given to the "winder" (the leading horse of a plough team).[33] In some areas, this custom transferred early to New Year or

---

[31] McIlwraith, Euan, and Stephen, Mark, https://www.bbc.co.uk/sounds/play/p0bcbsqh.
[32] Black and Thomas, *County Folk-Lore: Orkney and Shetland*, p. 198.
[33] *Scots Weekly Magazine, 1832-33*, p. 51.

Handsel Monday:[34] Robert Burns alludes to this in "The Auld Farmer's New-Year-Morning Salutation To His Auld Mare, Maggie".

A drunken season followed. By custom, in households with a large enough fireplace to accommodate a Yule log (usually cut from an ash tree [35]), even servants on duty were permitted to take ale with every meal while the log burned – which could be for days.[36] In the Shetlands, even children were expected to take a nip of whisky before dawn to toast Yule morning.[37] Medieval beverages such as mead and heather ale, out of fashion for the rest of the year, remained festive favourites in many parts of the country.[38] Even in the 1830s, decades into the decline of Christmas observance on the mainland, the wassail-bowl of spiced wine or ale was passed round for almost a fortnight in the Hebrides; curiously, roasted eggs were

---

[34] Simpson, Evelyn Blantyre, *Folk Lore in Lowland Scotland* (London, 1908), p. 23.
[35] Ibid., pp. 155-56.
[36] *Scots Weekly Magazine, 1832-33*, p. 51.
[37] Black and Thomas, *County Folk-Lore: Orkney and Shetland*, p. 198.
[38] Simpson, *Folk Lore in Lowland Scotland*, p. 24.

sometimes substituted for the apples which bobbed in the bowl. [39] To enter a neighbour's house on New Year's Morning without a gift of drink was frowned upon; ale was traditionally preferred in the countryside, and whisky in the towns.[40]

Whisky may have had a festive association since it was first invented. The first recorded distiller of spirits in Scotland, the Dominican friar John Cor,[41] was paid fourteen shillings by King James IV at Christmas 1488, [42] and given the black livery of a royal clerk for Christmas 1494:[43] it is quite likely that he was being rewarded for furnishing the royal table with drink for the festivities.

Despite the fact that the English Christmas revival of the 1840s largely

---

[39] *Schoolmaster, Vol. 2*, p. 296.

[40] Ibid., p. 386.

[41] Burnett, George (ed.), *Exchequer Rolls of Scotland*, v. 10 (Edinburgh, 1887), p. 487: Brother John was given eight bolls of malt to make aqua vitae on 1st June 1495, the first recorded reference to malted liquor, but was likely already in the business.

[42] *Accounts of the Lord High Treasurer of Scotland*, v. 1 (Edinburgh, 1877), p. 100.

[43] Ibid., p. 232.

passed Scotland by, there were distinctive local recipes for plum pudding and mince pies, and even roastit bubblyjock – roast turkey, traditionally stuffed with chestnuts. Janet Warren in *A Feast of Scotland* [44] associates all of these with Yule, though it is likely that the seasonal associations of bubblyjock, at least, were weak before the 1960s.

Come Hogmanay, more baking would be necessary. It was customary for children to go about in the morning, "swaddled in a great sheet, doubled up in front, so as to form a vast pocket"[45], begging comestibles – traditionally but not invariably oatcakes – at the doors of the well-off.

> "My feet's cauld, my shoon's done,
> Gie's my cakes, and let's rin,"[46]

they sang. (In Fife, this custom persisted into the twentieth century, although by the

---

[44] Warren, Janet, *A Feast of Scotland*, London, 1990, pp. 165-67; Thomson, George L., *Traditional Scottish Recipes* (Edinburgh, 1976), p. 36.
[45] Chambers, *Popular Rhymes*, p. 164.
[46] Simpson, *Folk Lore in Lowland Scotland*, p. 22.

late nineteenth the oatcakes had been replaced with a dole of money.[47])

The term "Hogmanay" applied to each portion of these cakes as well as to the day itself, though its origin has never been satisfactorily explained. Chambers cites two proposed French origins – "au gueux menez", meaning "bring to the beggars", and "au gui menez", "go to the mistletoe". The applicability of the former is obvious; the latter, which Chambers favoured, was reportedly a cry of Christmas mummers in France. [48] The practice of begging for

---

[47] Simpkins, *County Folk-Lore: Fife*, p. 142.
[48] The "au gui menez" theory was first propounded by John Robison, most notorious today for his 1797 work *Proofs of a Conspiracy against all the Religions and Governments of Europe*, which remains influential in conspiracy theorist and anti-Masonic circles. Chambers later proposed several other possible origins, including *homme est né* ("(a) man is born"), and *hoggu-nott*, a reported Scandinavian term for the eve of Yule, referring to the slaughter of animals that night for the next day's feast. He also quoted several foreign equivalents – Hagmenu or Hagmena in Northern England, Aguilanneu in Touraine, Hoguinano in Normandy, and the Spanish Aguinaldo, which

comestibles had likely been transferred from Yule Een, to which it was still attached very late in the northern Highlands, with guisers and carollers being regaled with bread, butter, and crowdie (soft curd cheese).[49] In the Northern Isles, meanwhile, it was generally on New Year's Day that the companies of children would circulate, singing the "Neuer Sang", and with one of their number designated as the "Kyerrin Horse" who would carry the

---

referred to Christmas gifts. (Chambers, *Book of Days*, vol. 2, p. 788.)

An old song from Richmond, Yorkshire, uses the term "Hagman heigh":

To-night it is the New Year's night, to-morrow is the day,
And we are come for our right and for our ray,
As we used to do in old King Henry's day.
Sing, fellows, sing Hagman heigh!

(Henderson, *Notes on the folklore of the northern counties*, p. 77.)

[49] Carmichael, Alexander, *Carmina Gadelica* (3v., Edinburgh, 1900), Vol. I, pp. 126-27.

basket in which their dole of food and drink would be deposited.[50]

Black bun, a thick packing of dried fruit and spices in a thin crust of hard pastry, was and remains a Hogmanay favourite.[51] On the savoury side, Warren cites kipper cream – a sort of blancmange of flaked fish – as another dish of this season.[52] Hogmanay guisers in Fife and Lothian were treated to bread, cheese, shortbread, currant loaf, and three-cornered biscuits by their hosts, with whisky for the adults in the company, and ginger cordial for the children.[53] First-

---

[50] Towrie, Sigurd, https://www.orkneyjar.com/tradition/calendar/index.html.

[51] It may have begun as a Twelfth Night king-cake of the kind popular in much of Continental Europe. King-cakes formed part of the celebrations at the court of the French-raised Queen Mary, who apparently introduced them to Scotland: Douglas, Hugh, *The Hogmanay Companion* (2nd edition) (Glasgow, 2000), pages unnumbered.

[52] Warren, *A Feast of Scotland*, pp. 168-69. See Thomson, *Traditional Scottish Recipes*, p. 38, for another black bun recipe.

[53] *Folk-lore*, v. 4 (1893), p. 313.

footers the next day (or on Handsel Monday), meanwhile, were expected to *bring* comestibles – not just the whisky which remains traditional, but buns, shortbread, broken biscuits, and often ginger wine or a "het pint" of spiced ale with eggs whisked through it; [54] in the Highlands, Atholl brose – a strained mix of whisky, oatmeal, and honey – was the preferred morning drink. [55] In Galloway, first-footers did not await the dawn, but brought their het pints at midnight: [56] toasting the New Year from a wassail bowl as the bells rang was a custom in many parts, and remains so in some. New Year's guests in the Orkneys would receive bread,

---

[54] Simpkins, *County Folk-Lore: Fife*, p. 147; Thomson, *Traditional Scottish Recipes*, p. 11. It was explicitly in order that the poor of Lanark might buy a het pint that Lord Carmichael set up a fund in 1662 to disburse cash every New Year's Day. (Urquhart, *Statistical Account*, vol. 15 (1795), p. 44.)

[55] Warren, *A Feast of Scotland*, pp. 169-70; Thomson, *Traditional Scottish Recipes*, p. 24.

[56] Cromek, R. H., *Remains of Nithsdale and Galloway Song: with Historical Notices relative to the Manners and Customs of the Peasantry* (London, 1810), p. 41.

ale, beef, or a smoked goose.[57] In parts of Angus and Aberdeenshire in the nineteenth century, even far from the sea, there was a tradition of dressing herring up in crepe paper skirts and bonnets and presenting them to neighbours on New Year's Day: the origins of this curious custom have so far eluded detection.[58]

Feasting and drinking continued until Handsel Monday, when ale would be freshly brewed: the yeastiness of which was credited by one William Hunter, a formerly bedridden coal miner in Tillicoultry, with effecting an instant and permanent cure of his hitherto disabling rheumatism when his neighbours persuaded him to get drunk with them on Handsel Monday of 1738.[59] In Perth, even the poorest families enjoyed a leg of lamb on Handsel Monday, though it might be the only butcher meat they tasted all year.[60]

---

[57] Black and Thomas, *County Folk-Lore: Orkney and Shetland*, p. 195.
[58] http://angusfolklore.blogspot.com/2019/12/yule-and-hogmanay-revelstraditions.html.
[59] Chambers, *Book of Days*, v. 1, p. 52.
[60] Penny, George, *Traditions of Perth* (Perth, 1836), p. 142.

Celebrations lasted still longer in the Northern Isles, where Yule did not fully end until Twenty-Fourth Night; only then, finally, did Presbyterian austerity reassert itself, and Scotland sober up.

## 2: *Sports and games*

> "Has ne'er in a' this countra been,
> Sic shoudering and sic fa'ing,
> As happen'd but few ouks sinsyne,
> Here at the Christmas Ba'ing."[61]

Traditions varied as to what should be done after supping brose on Yule morning. The fairy tale "The Ridire of Grianaig[62] and

---

[61] Skinner, John, "The Monymusk Christmas Ba'ing"; in *Amusements of Leisure Hours: or Poetical Pieces, Chiefly in the Scottish Dialect* (Edinburgh, 1809), p. 41. Skinner allegedly wrote this celebration of rough Yuletide football in Aberdeenshire in 1739, when he was only eighteen years old. It is often cited as the oldest surviving piece of Doric literature.

[62] Literally, the Knight of Greenock: Campbell argues that *ridire* could refer to an ancient petty king, or that he could be a more supernatural figure, a "Knight of the Sun" – *Grian* being a term for the sun likely deriving from the name of a solar goddess in Goidelic paganism. The story itself shows elements of solar / seasonal myth – the Ridire's overwhelming grief for his kidnapped daughters being connected to midwinter carries obvious echoes of Demeter mourning the abduction of Persephone,

Iain the Soldier's Son", collected in Islay in 1859, begins with the hero and his brothers celebrating Christmas Day with a game of shinty: the fact that they play on the eponymous knight's land without permission, disturbing his grief over his kidnapped daughters, is the catalyst for the beginning of Iain's adventures.[63] That this is a commonplace part of festivities seems to be taken for granted; collector John Francis Campbell remarks that shinty matches on a huge scale had until the early nineteenth century been a regular part of

---

especially when the solar associations of his title are taken into account: and her kidnappers are giants, associated in Scotland as in Scandinavia with winter and foul weather, who have taken her underground in the far west, making one think of the setting of the sun. Possibly we have here a long-remembered myth of the origins of winter, and Iain's rescue of the girls – his quest beginning at the Winter Solstice, when the days start to lengthen, and ending at Beltane – explains how spring came to be restored.

[63] Campbell, John Francis, *Popular Tales of the West Highlands, Volume III* (Paisley and London, 1890), pp. 9-10; see also *New Statistical Account*, vol. 14, p. 223.

the season in the Hebrides, with teams of hundreds taking part in the great match on New Year's Day, and goal-scorers celebrated as heroes.[64] In Inverness, the *New Statistical Account* noted that Christmas was the one time of year when shinty and other once commonplace sports[65] were still practised, having been driven from the rest of the year by "the sober realities and industrious habits of the present age".[66]

In Angus in the latter part of the eighteenth century, women would visit their friends while men engaged in shooting competitions, the master marksman winning a prize made for the

---

[64] Ibid., p. 28. The match at Rosneath in Argyll was particularly celebrated, even after this time, attended with music and banners and prepared for months in advance: Guthrie, E. J., *Old Scottish Customs: local and general* (London and Glasgow, 1885), p. 105.

[65] Including football, bowls, shot-putting, and hammer-throwing.

[66] *New Statistical Account*, vol. 14, p. 19. In Sutherland, too, it was noted that old amusements lingered on at Christmas and New Year, which had once been commonplace regardless of the season.

occasion.[67] Come evening they would repair to the public house for raffles, cards, hard drinking, and general revelry. At St Fergus in Aberdeenshire in the same era, masters and servants together would go to play golf on the Links as equals.[68] Shooting competitions were popular in the Highlands too, along with ball games; while younger children played on swings exchanging shouts of "I'll eat your kale!" – "You shan't eat my kale!"[69]

By the twentieth century, the Angus shooting competitions had been displaced to New Year's Day, and the handmade prize replaced with cash – or, in Montrose, a joint of beef or pork.[70] Meanwhile, children too young to shoot competed at the tee-totum, spinning tops for prizes of nuts.[71]

---

[67] Anonymous correspondent to the *Literary and Statistical Magazine for Scotland* (Edinburgh, 1819); see also Sinclair, *Statistical Account*, vol. 2 (1792), p. 509.
[68] *New Statistical Account*, vol. 12, p. 198.
[69] *Scots Weekly Magazine 1832-33*, p. 53.
[70] Coleman, Keith, http://angusfolklore.blogspot.com/2019/12/yule-and-hogmanay-revelstraditions.html
[71] Ibid.

In the eighteenth century, Hogmanay and New Year's Day were known as the *Daft Days* for their "frantic merriment". Robert Fergusson celebrated this in his 1772 poem of the same name:

> "Let mirth abound, let social cheer
> Invest the dawning of the year;
> Let blithesome innocence appear
> To crown our joy;
> Nor envy wi sarcastic sneer
> Our bliss destroy."[72]

By the 1820s, as Robert Chambers primly remarked, "these follies [were] much corrected".[73] (The journal *Folk-lore* would later recall Chambers' time of writing as an era when the whisky-shops were still open all night in Edinburgh, and midnight of the New Year the occasion of "rioting and fighting", in particular between the city's bakers and students of the University.[74] The traditional gathering of young men at

---

[72] Fergusson, Robert, *The Works of Robert Fergusson; with a short account of his life, and a concise glossary* (Edinburgh, 1805), p. 124.
[73] Chambers, *Popular Rhymes*, p. 161.
[74] *Folk-lore*, v. 4 (1893), pp. 310-11.

the Tron Church ahead of midnight to go first-footing, often after much drink had already been taken, perhaps made such conflicts inevitable. In 1812, a "small party of reckless boys" took advantage of the chaos to attack and rob as many first-footers as they could; two of their victims died of injuries sustained and three of the perpetrators were later executed. The celebrations went into a steep decline thereafter.[75])

At Ravenscraig Castle in Fife, the villagers of Pathhead would gather on Handsel Monday to play *kyles*: attempting to roll a ball through an upright iron hoop or into a hole, and betting on the outcome. At the Court Cave in nearby Wemyss, the game of the day was *yettlings*, the aim being to roll an iron or whinstone ball from one goal to the other in the smallest number of throws.[76]

Further north at Cullen Bay, a procession of young folk would leave the town every Yule Day, with a piper at their head, to play upon the sands at football, races, bowls (played with a cannonball!),

---

[75] Chambers, *Book of Days*, v. 1, p. 29.
[76] Simpkins, *County Folk-Lore: Fife*, pp. 149-51.

throwing the hammer, and many another diversion. "The games", we are told,

> "were keenly contested, and the victor was crowned by a bonnet adorned with feathers and ribbons… When the games were over, the whole parties had a dance on the green, with that merriment and glee, to which the etiquette and formation of the ball-room at the present day are total strangers."

They would then process back to town for a more formal ball, presided over by the victor in his bonnet.[77]

But the most famous seasonal diversions are the Yuletide football matches still played to this day in the Northern Isles. The best known of these is the Kirkwall Ba', played in the streets of Orkney's main town on Yule Day and New

---

[77] *New Statistical Account*, vol. 13, pp. 331-32. Similar games took place at Halloween; however, by the Victorian era, both had declined considerably.

Year.[78] The teams are "Uppies" (traditionally those born "Up the Gate", south of Kirkwall Cathedral) and "Doonies" (born "Doon the Gate", to the north): though team membership has now become effectively hereditary, families remaining Uppies or Doonies even if they have long since moved to another part of town. Boys play in the morning and men in the afternoon, the games sometimes overlapping: the aim is simply to reach the goal (a wall in the Doonie end of town for the Uppies, the sea for the Doonies), a chosen player from the first team to score being awarded the coveted ball itself: but with very large teams, confined spaces, and few rules, matches can last several hours, and often night falls before the ba' is won.[79]

---

[78] Towrie, orkneyjar.com/tradition/bagame/index.html
[79] Ibid.; cf. Shrovetide football matches in England, and Campbell's account of New Year's shinty in the Hebrides (above).

## 3: *Songs and carols*

Scotland has always been rich in folk songs and rhymes, and there are many associated with the Christmas season, when the very bees were popularly believed to sing in their hives.[80] Fife folk even referred to Hogmanay as "Singen-Een". [81] The northern Highlands and Hebrides possessed many a Gaelic carol for both Yule Een and Hogmanay; the chorus *Ho righ! Beannaicht e!* ("Ho, the King! Blessed is he!") featured prominently in several of the former.[82] And, of course, "Auld Lang Syne" and "A Guid New Year" remain favourites to see the new year in.

Despite the fact that the Twelve Days of Christmas were not demarcated in early modern Scotland, Epiphany being little celebrated after the Reformation, the country possessed its own version of the eponymous carol – though it in fact features thirteen days, to include Epiphany

---

[80] *Schoolmaster, Vol. 2*, p. 385.
[81] Simpkins, *County Folk-Lore: Fife*, pp. 141-42.
[82] Carmichael, op. cit., Vol. I, pp. 126-37.

(6th January) itself. Unlike the more familiar version, the numbers of the gifts confusingly failed to match the days; and the final gift was the rather anticlimactic "three stalks of merry corn" (though these might stand for John Barleycorn, and therefore for whisky or ale, a perhaps more appealing Christmas present).

## THE YULE DAYS[83]

*The king sent his lady on the first Yule-day
A papingo-aye;
Wha learns my carol and carries it away?*

*The king sent his lady on the second Yule-day
Three partridges, a papingo-aye;
Wha learns my carol and carries it away?*

*The king sent his lady on the third Yule-day
Three plovers, three partridges, a papingo-aye;
Wha learns my carol and carries it away?*

*The king sent his lady on the fourth Yule-day
A goose that was grey,
Three plovers, three partridges, a papingo-aye;
Wha learns my carol and carries it away?*

*The king sent his lady on the fifth Yule-day
Three starlings, a goose that was grey,
Three plovers, three partridges, a papingo-aye;
Wha learns my carol and carries it away?*

*The king sent his lady on the sixth Yule-day
Three goldspinks, three starlings, a goose that was grey,
Three plovers, three partridges, a papingo-aye;*

---

[83] Chambers, *Popular Rhymes*, pp. 42-43.

*Wha learns my carol and carries it away?*

*The king sent his lady on the seventh Yule-day*
*A bull that was brown,*
*Three goldspinks, [etcetera]*
*Three plovers, three partridges, a papingo-aye;*
*Wha learns my carol and carries it away?*

*The king sent his lady on the eighth Yule-day*
*Three ducks a-merry laying,*
*A bull that was brown, [etcetera]*
*Three plovers, three partridges, a papingo-aye;*
*Wha learns my carol and carries it away?*

*The king sent his lady on the ninth Yule-day*
*Three swans a-merry swimming,*
*Three ducks a-merry laying, [etcetera]*
*Three plovers, three partridges, a papingo-aye;*
*Wha learns my carol and carries it away?*

*The king sent his lady on the tenth Yule-day*
*An Arabian baboon,*
*Three swans a-merry swimming, [etcetera]*
*Three plovers, three partridges, a papingo-aye;*
*Wha learns my carol and carries it away?*

*The king sent his lady on the eleventh Yule-day*
*Three hinds a-merry hunting,*
*An Arabian baboon, [etcetera]*
*Three plovers, three partridges, a papingo-aye;*

> *Wha learns my carol and carries it away?*
>
> *The king sent his lady on the twelfth Yule-day*
> *Three maids a-merry dancing,*
> *Three hinds a-merry hunting, [etcetera]*
> *Three plovers, three partridges, a papingo-aye;*
> *Wha learns my carol and carries it away?*
>
> *The king sent his lady on the thirteenth Yule-day*
> *Three stalks of merry corn,*
> *Three maids a-merry dancing, [etcetera]*
> *Three plovers, three partridges, a papingo-aye;*
> *Wha learns my carol and carries it away?*

In modern times, a delightful Scoticised version of the familiar English carol has been created: *The 12 Days o Yule*, whose gifts range from "12 drummers dirlin" to "a reid robin in a rowan tree".[84]

The children who went begging for oatcakes on Hogmanay also had a variety of rhymes to chant as they went about.

> "Hogmanay,
> Trollolay,

---

[84] Rennie, Susan, and Land, Matthew, *The 12 Days o Yule* (Edinburgh, 2015).

Give us of your white bread, and none of your grey!"

"Get up, goodwife, and shake your feathers,
And dinna think that we are beggars;
For we are bairns come out to play,
Get up and gie's our Hogmanay!"

"Get up, goodwife, and binna sweer,
And deal your bread to them that's here;
For the time will come when ye'll be dead,
And then ye'll neither need ale nor bread."

"My shoon are made of hoary hide,
Behind the door I downa bide;
My tongue is sair, I daurna sing –
I fear I will get little thing."

"My feet's cauld, my shoon's thin;
Gie's my cakes, and let me rin!"

"Roond the midden I whuppit a geese:
I'll sing nae mair till I get a bit piece."[85]

---

[85] Chambers, *Popular Rhymes*, pp. 165-66; Simpkins, *County Folk-Lore: Fife*, p. 142.

Campbell records that, in the Highlands, Hogmanay rhymes were peppered with the names of mythological personages from the Ossianic cycle: though sadly he gives no details.[86]

In Orkney, meanwhile, Hogmanay guisers had their own whole carol, which even after three hundred years of Protestantism preserved a memory of devotion to the Virgin Mary. The earliest surviving version is partially reconstructed by a correspondent of Chambers, but for what it's worth, goes as on the left below; a few decades later, Robert Menzies Fergusson collected the longer version on the right.

| "This night it is guid New'r E'en's night, We're a' here Queen Mary's men; And we're come here to crave our right, And that's before our lady. | "Peace be to this buirdly biggin'! We're a' Queen Mary's men, From the stethe unto the riggin', And that's before our Lady. This is gude New |

---

[86] Campbell, op. cit., p. 28.

The very first thing
which we do crave,
We're a' here Queen
Mary's men;
A bonny white
candle we must
have,
And that's before
our lady.

Goodwife, gae to
your butter ark,
And weigh us here
ten mark –
Ten mark, ten pund;
Look that ye grip
weel to the grund.

Goodwife, gae to
your geelin vat,
And fetch us here a
skeel o' that.

Gang to your
awmrie, gin ye
please,
And bring frae there
a yow-milk cheese;
And syne bring here

Year's even nicht –
We're a' Queen
Mary's men;
An' we've come to
claim our richt,
And that's before
our Lady.

The morrow is gude
New Year's day –
We're a' Queen
Mary's men;
An' we've come
here to sport and
play,
And that's before
our Lady.

The hindmost house
that we came from –
We're a' Queen
Mary's men;
We gat oat-cake and
sowen's scone;
The three-lugged
coo was standing
fou:
We hope to get the
same from you,

a sharping-stane,
We'll sharp our whittles ilka ane.

Ye'll cut the cheese, and eke the round,
But aye take care ye cutna your thoom.

Gae fill the three-pint cog o' ale,
The maut maun be aboon the meal.
We houp your ale is stark and stout,
For men to drink the auld year out.

Ye ken the weather's snaw and sleet,
Stir up the fire to warm our feet.
Our shoon's made o' mare's skin,
Come open the door, and let's in."[87]

And that's before our Lady.

Gudewife, gae to your kebbock-creel,
We're a' Queen Mary's men,
And see thou count the kebbocks weel,
And that's before our Lady.

Gudewife, gae to your gealding-vat
An' let us drink till our lugs crack,
An' fetch us ane an' fetch us twa,
An' aye the merrier we'll gang awa',
And that's before our Lady.

Gudewife, gae to your butter-ark –
We're a' Queen Mary's men;

---

[87] Chambers, *Popular Rhymes*, pp. 167-68.

An' fetch us here ten
bismar mark;
See that ye grip
weel in the dark,
And that's before
our Lady.

May a' your mares
be weel to foal –
We're a' Queen
Mary's men,
And every ane be a
staig foal,
And that's before
our Lady.

May a' your kye be
weel to calve –
We're a' Queen
Mary's men;
And every ane a
queyoch calf,
And that's before
our Lady.

May a' your ewes be
weel to lamb –
We're a' Queen
Mary's men;

And every ane a
ewe and a ram,
And that's before
our Lady.

May a' your hens
rin in a reel –
We're a' Queen
Mary's men;
And every ane twal
at her heel,
And that's before
our Lady.

Here we hae brocht
our carrying-horse
We're a' Queen
Mary's men;
An' mony a curse
licht on his corse;
He'll eat mair meat
than we can get;
He'll drink mair
drink than we can

|  | swink, And that's before our Lady."[88] |
|--|--|

Meanwhile, the Shetland fiddle tune "Day Dawn" was traditionally to be played on Yule morning, and at no other time of year.[89] It was similarly considered ill luck in the twentieth century to sing "For It's Hogmanay" at any time but the eponymous night – including failing to finish it before midnight.[90] (The latter song ends with a bittersweet reminder that "We can't foresee / Where we all shall be / On the next Hogmanay": all the more poignant when one remembers its likely origins in the trenches of World War One.[91])

Before departing their hosts' house, Dunfermline guisers would sing:

---

[88] Fergusson, Robert Menzies, *Rambles in the Far North* (London, 1884), pp. 170-71.

[89] Black and Thomas, *County Folk-Lore: Orkney and Shetland*, p. 204.

[90] McIlwraith and Stephen, https://www.bbc.co.uk/sounds/play/p0bcbsqh.

[91] Foster, Henry Clapham, *At Antwerp and the Dardanelles* (London, 1918), p. 16.

> "God bless the master of this house,
> And mistress also,
> Likewise the little bairnies,
> That round the table go,
> May your purse be full of money,
> Your cellars full of beer,
> We wish you many a Hogmanay,
> And many a good New Year,"

or:

> "Blinking Jock the cobbler,
> He had a blinking e'e;
> He selt his wife for a hunder pounds,
> And that was a' his gear.
> His pockets fu' o' money,
> His barrels fu' o' beer;
> Please to help the Guisers,
> And I wish you a happy New Year."[92]

---

[92] Simpkins, *County Folk-Lore: Fife*, p. 143.

## 4: *Guising*

> "Here come the guisers,
> Never been before,
> Not to beg or borrow,
> But to drive away your sorrow."[93]

> "Onything for the guisers?" – "Nothing but a red-hot poker."[94]

Guisers are today associated with Halloween. Indeed, the American trick-or-treat probably originates from guising, though in Scotland treats are traditionally earned by singing or telling jokes rather than demanded with menaces. But historically, guisers (or guisards, as they used to be known) were much more strongly linked with the Christmas season. On Yule Day, Hogmanay, New Year's Day,

---

[93] Simpkins, *County Folk-Lore: Fife*, p. 143.
[94] Traditional exchange in Forfar, quoted by http://angusfolklore.blogspot.com/2019/12/yule-and-hogmanay-revelstraditions.html from Rodger, Jean, *Lang Strang* (Forfar, 1948).

and Handsel Monday (see below, chapter 6), and on Yule Een in the Highlands,[95] they would go from house to house soliciting money for their performances.[96]

Chambers describes them going about in pairs, always of two boys. The one with the better voice, in his father's shirt and wearing a paper hood and mask, would be preceded by the "Bessie", in girl's clothing and carrying a broomstick: and at each house from which they were not driven away, the masked boy would sing while the Bessie danced or japed.[97] In some parts, however, the details were much less prescribed. At Kennoway in Fife, "men and women, boys and girls, dressed themselves

---

[95] Carmichael, *Carmina Gadelica* vol. I, pp. 126-27. In Gaelic the French-origin word *guisers* was rendered "goisearan". They were also known in various parts of the Highlands as "fir dàn", verse-men; "gillean Nollaige", Yule lads; and "nuallairean", which Carmichael translates as "rejoicers".

[96] It has been suggested that the costumes of guisers originally represented fairies or other spirits which had to be appeased, hence the offerings made to them. See Norman, Mark, thefolklorepodcast.com, episode 50.

[97] Chambers, *Popular Rhymes*, pp. 169-70.

in strange costumes, and blackened their faces", and would perform as they pleased.[98]

Blackened faces, though they could have racial connotations, were also of course an effective means of disguise: an especially necessary measure in early modern Scotland, when the Kirk was doing its best to suppress guising. It was perhaps the most abominated of Yule customs, because it often involved cross-dressing: an investigation by the Stories of Scotland podcast in 2021, using the Kirk Sessions of Elgin, found that arrested guisers would admit dancing but deny wearing costumes, or admit to a woman's coat but not a skirt; and that the fine imposed for guising in drag was double that for a false beard.[99]

At Lerwick on Yule-Een, children and youths in "fantastic and gaudy costumes" paraded and begged long into the night, and at one o'clock in the morning would light a tar barrel and drag it blazing

---

[98] Simpkins, *County Folk-Lore: Fife*, p. 144.
[99] MacDonald and Johnstone, https://www.storiesofscotland.com/podcast/2021/12/21/bonus-christmas-crimes.

through the streets;[100] in the morning fiddlers would play and costumed revellers (dressed as "soldiers, sailors, Highlanders, Spanish Chevaliers, &c.") would be pulled along on makeshift chariots made from crates.[101] Brawls, the discharging of guns, and letting off explosives, were commonplace.[102] Similar displays followed at Hogmanay, when the guisers were led by a "gentleman" in cap and collar of straw, and at Uphelya or Up Helly Aa, originally the twenty-fourth day after Yule.

In later decades, as the local distinctiveness and supposed Norse roots

---

[100] Black and Thomas, *County Folk-Lore: Orkney and Shetland*, pp. 203-04. "Old Style" Yule and New Year, eleven days after the Gregorian date, continued to be observed in the Shetlands into the twentieth century. In fact, the calendars had drifted further apart by then: the current discrepancy is thirteen days, and has been since 1900/01: but the memory of the 1752 calendar shift died hard.
[101] Ibid., p. 204; the crates were passing out of use by the Edwardian era.
[102] McIlwraith and Stephen, https://www.bbc.co.uk/sounds/play/p0bcbsqh

of the festival became more emphasised, Viking costumes became the norm; a longship entered the festivities, borne on the shoulders and then set alight; and the tar barrels disappeared from earlier celebrations to become the sole preserve of Up Helly Aa, now celebrated on the last Tuesday in January. Attempts to ban the tar barrel in the 1870s proved ineffective, but probably contributed to the decline in its use at Yule and Hogmanay. The longship was introduced in 1889,[103] but a wild multiplicity of costume styles was the norm into at least the 1920s: the modern Up Helly Aa is almost entirely a late confection. Even today, it is only the main "squad" following the Guizer Jarl[104] who necessarily dress as Vikings. (It is commonplace for some of the other revellers to dress as the returning sailors who are said to have revived the semi-

---

[103] Derived from an earlier practice of setting a blazing fishing boat adrift at New Year: McIlwraith and Stephen, op. cit.

[104] The leader of the procession, in operatic pseudo-Norse armour: a character introduced in 1881.

moribund old custom in the Napoleonic era.)

It is hard to miss the similarity of the modern Up Helly Aa to a less famous custom, the Comrie Flambeaux. At midnight on Hogmanay, at Comrie in Perthshire, long torches are lit and paraded through the village to the sound of the pipes; and, like the Shetlanders, the locals compete to display the best fancy dress. (These days, the children have their own parade earlier in the evening.) [105] This custom may be ancient, as it is strikingly similar to St Obert's Eve in sixteenth century Perth. Held on the 10th of December – which was the eve of the Solstice in the Julian Calendar from 1500 to 1699 – this festivity also involved a torchlit procession through the city, preceded by pipers and drummers, and followed by costumed guisers. These included a devil in a long coat and a horse wearing a man's shoes; the whole affair was run by the city's bakers. After the Reformation, it was suppressed for being "blasphemous and

---

[105] http://www.comrie.org.uk/business-directory/125/comrie-flambeaux/.

heathenish", finally falling into disuse after several guisers were imprisoned in 1588.[106]

The tar barrel also has its mainland equivalents, most famously in the *clavie*, a custom from Burghead in Moray. Evelyn Simpson tells us:

> "… what was the origin of the word clavie, or the meaning of the belief adhering to it, no one knows. On Yule night, according to past dating, they make this unique clavie, *i.e.*, a barrel sawn in two, to the lower half of which there is affixed a long handle. In the manufacture of the clavie it is all-important that no iron hammer is to be used, but a stone does in its stead. The barrel is filled with wood dipped in tar and piled so as to form a pyramid with a hollow in it. Into the centre of the pyre is placed a burning peat. Another rule… is that no light

---

[106] Barrett, Michael, *A calendar of Scottish saints* (Fort Augustus, 1919), pp. 177-78.

be set to the tarry pile except by a brand already ablaze, and a modern match is sternly excluded. The clavie set aglow, a further libation of tar is poured upon it, and, regardless of flame and smoke, a man shoulders the flaring clavie. If he falls, or even stumbles, it augurs ill for the town, so a bearer strong thewed is carefully selected. When a bearer is wearied, or is choked by smoke, another is always there eager to carry the clavie. One after another they step forth until the town has been encompassed by the flaring barrel. Then they march to a hillock called the Doorie, where on a stone the remaining blaze is placed and more fuel added. In past centuries it was fed all night long till a new day dawned, but in this hurrying age… they let the fire burn on the altar but for a brief space and proceed to roll what remains of the smouldering barrel adown the western slope. On its last journey a scramble is made by the onlookers, for every one in the crowd wishes to seize a brand from the descending, dying clavie. Once secured, the possessor bears it home in triumph, for it is credited with the power of preserving those under the roof tree that shelters it from ill for a year. In bygone times one strong man was selected to carry the clavie around the town, but now the post of honour is shared among several of the able-bodied. Also in days of yore the ships in the harbour were visited by the clavie. Indeed as late as 1875 the clavie was carried on board one vessel about to make her first voyage. Grain was showered on her deck, and then with a sprinkling of fire and water she was named *Doorie*. The town has grown greatly and assumed bigger proportions than the fiery clavie can encircle, so only the older part is girded by the burning barrel."[107]

At Minnigaff in Galloway, too, blazing tar barrels were – well into the twentieth century – carried to the Hogmanay bonfire by the young men of the district, who would then dance round dressed as "giants, dwarfs, demons", and, for no particular discernible reason, Native Americans.[108]

Fire is, indeed, a key part of the celebrations in many parts of the country. At Biggar in Lanarkshire, December is spent gathering wood in the town centre for a great bonfire lit on Hogmanay; while at Stonehaven in Aberdeenshire on the same night, the Fireball Ceremony is held, a troop of revellers parading through the town swinging blazing balls around their

---

[107] Simpson, *Folk Lore in Lowland Scotland*, pp. 125-27. Today, the clavie is burned on the night of 11th January: the Julian date of Hogmanay at the time of the 1752 calendar shift. Simpson does not mention that the Doorie Hill is the site of an ancient Pictish fortress, which may be why it was chosen.

[108] McCormick, Andrew, *The Tinkler-Gypsies of Galloway* (Dumfries, 1906), p. 83.

heads, before hurling them into the harbour.[109]

Larger bands of guisers or "Yule Boys"[110] in Lowland Scotland would in former times perform not only songs, but a play, equivalent to the mummers' plays of England. The plot is the same as in England, but a personage called Galatian or Golashan is substituted for St George. (Galatian is sometimes identified with Calgacus, the Caledonian war leader who fought the Romans in the first century: I suspect the name may in fact derive ultimately from Gathelus or Goídel Glas, mythical progenitor of the Gaelic people. Whether the Gaels themselves had any equivalent to this play is not known: it is recorded right across the Lowlands but not in the Highlands.)

Like St George, Galatian seems to represent the dying and reviving King of the Year, found in sacred drama from the Eastern Mediterranean long before the

---

[109] McIlwraith and Stephen, https://www.bbc.co.uk/sounds/play/p0bcbsqh.
[110] Guthrie, *Old Scottish Customs*, p. 164. Also "quhite boys o Yule" from their white costumes.

Christian era.[111] He fights with the Black Knight, and falls, but is revived by a miraculous doctor and goes on to victory. The menacing Black Knight was portrayed in some areas as a Highlander, heavily whiskered and swathed in tartan: a suitably frightening figure for an early modern Lowland audience. Sir Walter Scott was reportedly very fond of this play, and made sure to see a performance every year.[112]

The age of this custom is difficult to pin down. As with the St George plays, no texts survive earlier than the eighteenth century, though vague earlier references exist. But the similarity to very ancient dramas is undeniable.

Sadly, Galatian is largely forgotten. By the late nineteenth century, the Yule Boys' performances had shrunk to a few almost

---

[111] Gaster, Theodor H., *Thespis: Ritual, Myth, and Drama in the Ancient Near East* (New York, 1961), *passim*. For a possible alternative view see Norman, Mark, thefolklorepodcast.com, episode 49. The terms "Oak King" and "Holly King" for the combatants, often cited as coming from ancient myth, were in fact invented by Robert Graves in 1948.

[112] Chambers, *Popular Rhymes*, pp. 170 ff.

incoherent lines;[113] they passed out of fashion soon afterwards, and while mummers are occasionally seen in modern Scotland, they generally use English texts and star St George. However, guisers in some parts of Scotland – at Halloween as well as Yule and Hogmanay – were known within living memory as "galoshans" or similar.[114] Inverclyde's Galoshans Festival, founded in 2015 to celebrate guising traditions, is linked not to the Yule season but to Halloween.[115]

Remarkably, the most American of Christmas masquerades, the department store Santa Claus, was the creation of a Scotsman. The flamboyant Edinburgh-born businessman and philanthropist James Edgar, who opened a dry goods store in Brockton, Massachusetts, in 1878, made costume performances a regular part of his marketing, performing as a clown, a sailor, or a First Nations chieftain: and in 1890 he had the happy inspiration of playing St

---

[113] Guthrie, op. cit.
[114] McIlwraith and Stephen, https://www.bbc.co.uk/sounds/play/p08xphs6.
[115] Ibid.

Nicholas. The performance proved hugely popular, and was soon copied in cities all over the United States, and ultimately across the world.[116]

---

[116] Park, Michael, https://bequiet.media/scotland-scottish-history-podcast.

## 5: *Superstition*

The entire Yule season was associated, all over Scotland, with a great many superstitious beliefs and practices. In the Shetlands, "the Yules", as the season was known, began with Tul-ya's Een, on 18th December.[117]

> "On that night the Trows received permission to leave their homes in the heart of the

---

[117] Sigurd Towrie suggests it may earlier have begun on Maunsmass Een – that is, 12th December, the eve of the feast of the islands' patron, St Magnus. Magnus' principal feast, however, was on 16th April. After the 1752 calendar shift, Shetlanders continued to observe Julian dates for many generations: interestingly, it seems that they did account for the further drift between the calendars in 1800, but not in 1900, celebrating Yule on 6th January (the Julian equivalent of 25th December between 1800 and 1899) until at least the First World War. See MacDonald and Johnstone, https://www.storiesofscotland.com/podcast/2022/12/22/trows-of-yuletide-shetlands-festive-folklore.

earth and dwell, if it so pleased them, above ground... One of the most important of all Yule-tide observances was the 'saining' required to guard life or property from the Trows...

"At day-set on Tul-ya's e'en two straws were plucked from the stored provender and laid, in the form of a cross, at the steggie leading to the yard... A hair from the tail of each cow... was plaited together and fastened over the byre door, and a 'lowing taand' was carried through the barn and other out-houses."[118]

Further precautions followed the next day, Helya's Night, with a prayer to the Virgin for the safety of children, which persisted centuries after the Reformation.

---

[118] Black and Thomas, *County Folk-Lore: Orkney and Shetland*, pp. 196-97. The accused witch Katherine Jonesdochter told a Shetland court in 1616 that she had witnessed the issuing forth of the trows: Dalyell, John Graham, *The darker superstitions of Scotland, illustrated from history and practice* (Edinburgh, 1834), pp. 532-33.

> "Mary midder had de haund
> Ower aboot for sleepin'-baund,
> Had da lass and had da wife,
> Had da bairn a' its life.
> Mary midder had de haund
> Round da infant's o' oor laund."[119]

Sigurd Towrie links the association of Helya's Night with motherhood to Bede's assertion that the pagan Angles and Saxons had called 24th December "mothers' night"[120] – perhaps a stretch, but not necessarily so. It is, of course, also hard to miss the similarity of "Helya" and "Up Helly Aa", formerly called "Uphelya".

The 20th was Tammasmas Een, its night sacred to the Apostle Thomas, whose feast fell the following day: and neither work nor amusements of any kind were permitted after sunset, a ban which was scrupulously observed.

> "The very babe unborn

---

[119] Ibid., p. 197.
[120] Towrie, orkneyjar.com/tradition/yule/yule3.htm; Bede, *De Temporum Ratione*, XV.

> Cries oh dul! dul!
> For the breaking o' Thammasmas nicht,
> Five nichts afore Yule." [121]

This meant that a lot of work had to be done beforehand, as it was ill luck to greet Yule Day with an untidy house.[122] (That this is also usually the eve of the Winter Solstice in the Gregorian Calendar was probably a coincidence, despite the Norse heritage of the isles and the strength of tradition there: the calendar shift was not accepted in the U.K. until 1752, surely far too late to have influenced this custom.)

---

[121] Black and Thomas, *County Folk-Lore: Orkney and Shetland*, p. 197.

[122] Towrie, orkneyjar.com/tradition/yule/yule7.htm. Tammasmas Een had once been celebrated in Lowland Scotland, but this the Kirk had more successfully suppressed. In 1586, three men were imprisoned in Glasgow for "most superstitiously observing St Thomas's eve… with pipes and tambours to the trouble of sundry honest men in the town sleeping in their beds; and the raising of the old dregs of superstition used among the Papists". (Quoted in *New Statistical Account*, vol. 6. p. 928.)

On Yule Een itself, after the baking of the Yule-cakes, Shetlanders would wash themselves, dropping burning coals into the water to ward yet again against the power of the trows, before donning bedwear which was required to be clean and if possible new. [123] In the morning the gudeman would bless each member of the household with the words:

> "Yule gude and yule gear
> Follow de trew da year."[124]

Gifts of food and drink were left for the hogboon who haunted ancient burial mounds.[125]

---

[123] Black and Thomas, *County Folk-Lore: Orkney and Shetland*, p. 198. Cf. the Icelandic superstition that children without new clothes on Christmas Day risk being eaten by the Yule Cat.
[124] Ibid.
[125] Towrie, orkneyjar.com/tradition/yule/yule2.htm. A similar custom existed in the village of Myrelandhorn near Wick, where, until the decline of the season in the early nineteenth century, it was usual for every inhabitant to offer bread, cheese, and silver to the spirits at

That Yule Een was considered the last opportunity of devils and witches to wreak harm before the holy season made it feared in many parts of Scotland. Many a farmer would read passages from the Bible to his animals that night, to preserve them from such supernatural mischief.[126] On Islay, misbehaving children feared An Crom Dubh na Nollaig, the Crooked Dark One of Christmas, whose howling could be heard on the winter wind.[127] In Glen Callater it

---

Kirk o Moss before dawn on Yule Day. (*New Statistical Account*, vol. 15, p. 161.) Guthrie (*Old Scottish Customs*, pp. 171-72) compares this to the offerings of bread and cheese left at the Chapel of Tears in Wick on the Feast of the Holy Innocents (28th December), the children slaughtered by Herod searching for the infant Jesus, to whom the chapel was dedicated. This feast was otherwise not much observed in Scotland.

[126] Chambers, *Popular Rhymes*, pp. 170 ff. On New Year's Day, Highlanders would burn sprigs of juniper in the byre to sain their cattle: Guthrie, *Old Scottish Customs*, p. 228.

[127] McIlwraith and Stephen, https://www.bbc.co.uk/sounds/play/p0bcbsqh. In Irish lore, Crom Dubh is an alternative name for Crom Cruach, a pagan god said to have demanded large scale human sacrifice and

was said that music from the fairy mounds could be heard around that time, and woe betide any who stopped too long to listen; a story was told of one man who was trapped within a rath for a whole year, until Yule came round again and afforded an opportunity for his friend to rescue him.[128]

In the Shetlands, however, the whole Yule season remained dangerous. At Papa Stour, it was said that evil spirits would buffet even the strongest if they strayed beyond the town-dyke after noon on Yule Day; and all over the islands it was feared that the trows, who could never resist a dance, would take human form to infiltrate the dances universally held after sunset on Yule Day to carry off the unsained.[129] Deaths and mischances during Yule, especially of children, were commonly

---

to have been ultimately defeated by St Patrick. In Ireland, Crom Dubh's Sunday is the last Sunday before Lammastide / Lughnasa.

[128] Taylor, Elizabeth, *Braemar Highlands: Their Tales, Traditions and History* (Edinburgh, 1869), p. 38.

[129] Black and Thomas, *County Folk-Lore: Orkney and Shetland*, pp. 49, 199; Dalyell, *The darker superstitions of Scotland*, pp. 532-33.

blamed on a lack of supernatural precautions. At the end of the festivities on Twenty-fourth Night, children were blessed once more, passages from the Bible read aloud, and cold iron displayed outside houses to banish trow and elf.[130]

Alan Temperley, writing in *The Scots Magazine* in the 1970s, recorded a Galloway tale that "St Ringan" (i.e. St Ninian, traditionally supposed to have evangelised the southern Picts in the early fifth century[131]) visited the province every Yule Een on his way to Bethlehem. He tells a story of the saint appearing as a beggar to a forlorn shepherd boy, and helping him to find and rescue a lost ewe in exchange for a bowl of kail brose – and records the line of oral transmission by which the story had reached him, back to the shepherd boy himself, who he suggests would have lived in the late sixteenth century.[132]

---

[130] Ibid., p. 203.

[131] It is now thought likely that "Ninian" is a character spun out of a clerical error: a duplicate of the sixth century Irish saint Finnian of Moville.

[132] Temperley, Alan, *Tales of Galloway* (London, 1979), pp. unnumbered.

In Angus, according to an anonymous writer in *The Scots Weekly Magazine* in 1833, the first member of a household to open the door on Yule morning and "let in Yule" would be the luckiest of their family for the year to come.[133] The article even indicates that some houses would leave the door open, with a table or chair in the gap set with bread and cheese for passers-by: surely not a good idea in a Scottish midwinter.

At Killin in Perthshire, seven stones blessed by St Fillan were kept at the mill, to which the sick resorted to be healed by the saint's power: but they had to be tended to, and every Yule Een a fresh bed of straw and river weeds was made up for each stone to lie in.[134] In parts of the North-East, the fire was smoored on Yule Een and re-lit from twigs of seven different woods – alder, ash, birch, hawthorn, hazel, rowan, and willow.[135] Borderers, by contrast,

---

[133] *Scots Weekly Magazine, 1832-33*, p. 51.
[134] *New Statistical Account*, v. 10, p. 1088.
[135] McIlwraith and Stephen, https://www.bbc.co.uk/sounds/play/p0bcbsqh.

deemed it very unlucky to let the fire go out on Yule Een or Hogmanay.[136]

To spin on Yule Day, or even to leave any wool or flax on the wheel on Yule-Een, was considered ill luck across Scotland; it was believed that any yarn left there would be spun up by the Devil and the reels would follow the spinner to church on her wedding day. To prevent this, any wool or flax which *was* left inadvertently upon the wheel had to be sprinkled with salt, before being cut away from the wheel instead of spun or lifted off.[137]

In the Shetlands, this was taken further, and work of any kind was forbidden:

> "Nedder bake nor brew,
> Shape nor shew,
> Upon gude Yule,
> Else muckle dul

---

[136] Henderson, *Notes on the folklore of the northern counties*, p. 72. The fire was similarly preserved at Beltane, Midsummer, and Halloween. Henderson notes that the more northerly practice of dousing and relighting the fire was paralleled in Germany.

[137] Black and Thomas, *County Folk-Lore: Orkney and Shetland*, p. 203.

> Will be dy share
> Dis year and mair."

At least this rhyme indicates that the person breaking the ban would live "dis year and mair" to suffer the "muckle dul"; but a story was told of a girl who, having been commissioned by a local laird to knit him a pair of socks, took up her needles upon Yule Day and died within months.[138] This ban on work persisted until New Year, the following rhyme being attributed to a hippocampus (mer-horse) which rose from the sea to rebuke men for fishing on the 28th:

> "Man wha fished in Yule week
> Fortune never mair did seek."[139]

On New Year's Day, at least some token work was expected, "to begin the year weel": at least in the Northern Isles. In other parts of the country, the Yule prohibition on work applied equally or more strongly to New Year, so spinning wheels and other instruments of domestic

---

[138] Ibid., p. 199.
[139] Ibid., p. 202.

labour were packed away on Hogmanay to avoid the temptation.[140]

Also unlucky was to let the Yule log burn out before Yule Day was done. Poorer households, where the log was not a practical possibility, would acquire instead a massive candle, to which the same beliefs applied.[141]

In Fife, it was customary to bring in water, corn, and kale – the latter two surely unseasonable unless they had been laid by for the purpose – first thing on Yule morning, and failure to do so was believed to lay up ill luck for the year ahead. Similarly, the "cream" of the well (i.e. water skimmed from the surface) was brought in immediately after midnight on Hogmanay.[142] In Aberdeenshire, a handful of grass was brought in as well, to ensure plentiful food for both animals and humans in the year ahead; and peat from the stack, to ensure plenty of fuel.[143]

Hogmanay, even more than Yule, has always been associated with ritualised

---

[140] Simpson, *Folk Lore in Lowland Scotland*, p. 23.
[141] *Scots Weekly Magazine, 1832-33*, p. 52.
[142] Simpkins, *County Folk-Lore: Fife*, p. 140.
[143] *Folklore*, vol. 4 (1893), p. 316.

festive customs, some of which persist to this day. My grandfather, a Perthshire farmer, used to fire his shotgun at midnight to scare away bad luck. At Auchterderran in Fife, it was considered a propitious day for weddings; [144] we've already mentioned the chanting children begging for oatcakes. In the Highlands, it was adults who made a circuit of their community requesting food, and did so after dark: but this custom incorporated strange elements of forgotten origin, with a strong pagan taste to them.

One of the party would drag behind them a dried cow's hide (an item long associated with prophecy and Druidry in Celtic tradition), which the rest would beat with sticks while chanting an abstruse Gaelic rhyme, some versions referring repeatedly to the *Cailleach*. This is a word of flexible meaning – it can refer to a hag, witch, or giantess, or simply an old woman, or even a nun. But it also referred to the *Cailleach Bheur*, the creator goddess in what little survives of Highland Gaelic mythology – and, significantly, the goddess of winter. "Spit in her two eyes, spit in her

---

[144] Simpkins, op. cit., p. 146.

stomach," they chanted: perhaps this referred to driving out winter as the new year came in.[145]

When welcomed into a house, the party would invent rhymes on the spot in praise of their hosts, and be "plentifully regaled with bread, butter, cheese, and whisky", before another piece of obscure ritual followed:

> "Before leaving the house, one of the party burns the breast part of the skin of a sheep, and puts it to the nose of every one, that all may smell it, as a charm against witchcraft and every infection."[146]

The equivalent Hogmanay circuit at Deerness in the Orkneys lacked the various ritual uses of animal skins, though it was otherwise very similar. In the far north of the mainland, the ceremony of the hide remained attached to Yule Een, and the hide carried around was not a cow's but a

---

[145] Hogmanay itself was called *Callaig* in Gaelic; there may be a pun here.
[146] Chambers, *Popular Rhymes*, pp. 166-67.

pure white lamb's. A child of the household – or a doll if no actual child was available – would represent Christ, and be carried three times sunwise around the fire sitting on the hide, while a hymn of praise was sung, before being offered homage.[147]

First-footing, the custom whereby the first guest to knock at the door on New Year's morning is expected to bring coal and whisky, and enter the house with their right foot leading, is not yet completely abandoned; nor is the superstition that the luckiest first-footer to welcome is a tall black-haired man, while red hair is unlucky.[148] (The prejudice against red hair may be due to the popular association of the colour with "bloody red Danes", and therefore go back to the Viking Age; the

---

[147] Carmichael, op. cit., pp. 126-27.
[148] In Victorian Angus, it was commonplace to arrange first-footing beforehand to avoid an unlucky visitor: the county was considered most unusual in having no prejudice against a woman as first-foot. *Folk-lore*, vol. 3 (1892), pp. 256-62; quoted by Coleman, http://angusfolklore.blogspot.com/2019/12/yule-and-hogmanay-revelstraditions.html. In Lothian, salt was also brought, as a symbol of good fortune.

fact that Scots are statistically far more likely to be red-headed than Scandinavians does not seem to have affected the stereotype. One might have thought an anti-Highland bias to be the more likely origin, were it not that the same superstition exists in the Highlands, and in Ireland.)[149]

More beliefs used to be associated with it: for instance, that the attributes of the first-footer would attach to the whole household for the year to come, one Auchterderran miner's wife blaming her husband's lateness for work on the fact that they had begun the year by welcoming a sleepy-eyed man.[150] (This might be why flat feet were considered an unlucky attribute in a first-footer in many parts of the country, one Galloway Traveller even blaming the loss of two horses in May on the flat-footed woman who had visited them in the New Year.)[151] In Edinburgh, it

---

[149] Norman, Mark, thefolklorepodcast.com, episodes 48 and 51; McIlwraith and Stephen, https://www.bbc.co.uk/sounds/play/p0bcbsqh.
[150] Simpkins, *County Folk-Lore: Fife*, p. 146.
[151] *Folk-lore*, vol. 3 (1892), p. 254; McCormick, *Tinkler-Gypsies*, p. 128.

was common in the eighteenth century for the daughter of the household to invite her sweetheart to be first-footer one year, and marry the following New Year's Day; by the late nineteenth, this custom had fallen out of use among the upper and middle classes, but was preserved by their servants. [152] This may be related to the Border superstition that the first person of the opposite sex seen by someone unmarried in the New Year would – if not in fact their future spouse – have the same first name.[153]

Where first-footers got their coal from is a question worth the asking, for on the feast nights of Yule, Hogmanay, and Handsel Monday, it was considered very *bad* luck to take coal *out* of one's own house, and believed that witches might make use of it against the original owner.[154] Perhaps some was left outside in advance of the season for this purpose. Fire, too, and iron, were not to be taken out of the house – beliefs paralleled at least as far afield as Rome and as far back as the early sixteenth

---

[152] *Folk-lore*, vol. 4 (1893), pp. 308-09.
[153] Henderson, op. cit., p. 73.
[154] *Scots Weekly Magazine 1832-33*, p. 51.

century.[155] To carry a knife or sharp tool into a house on New Year's Day, or to enter empty-handed, was considered very bad luck;[156] and to greet the new year with empty pockets or cupboards portended poverty in the year ahead. It was not unknown for people to borrow small sums of money over the season purely in order to avoid this fate; even Robert Burns once did so.[157]

Both Yule Een and Hogmanay are associated with tales of standing stones leaving their place and taking a walk. One such, at Birsay in Orkney, was said to take a drink at the Birsay Loch at midnight as the New Year came in: but to watch for it was reported to be extremely dangerous, and no local would attempt it. From the folklorist Robert Menzies Fergusson come stories of two outsiders who had attempted it within living memory: a student from Glasgow, who was found dazed and terrified the following morning, proclaiming that the stone had knocked him down, and who took weeks to recover;

---

[155] Henderson, op. cit., pp. 72-74.
[156] Rhys, op. cit., p. 256.
[157] Henderson, op. cit., p. 72.

and a shipwrecked sailor, who did not survive his vigil.[158]

A number of proverbs were associated with the season.

> "'Tween Martinmas and Yule,
> Water's wine in every pool"[159]

meant that rain between St Martin's Day (11th November) and Yule should be highly prized – a dubious assertion, as it was and is hardly a rare occurrence in Scotland. It was also widely and quite wrongly said that "a green Yule makes a fat kirkyard",[160] meaning that a mild Christmas portended a winter fatal to many; though some versions changed this to "a dark Yule". At least one Georgian-era sexton, Alexander Ouller of Logiealmond, considered a fat kirkyard something to aspire to, and had his own ritual of throwing his pick and shovel over the roof of the kirk every Yule-Een, to assure

---

[158] Fergusson, *Rambles in the Far North*, pp. 53-55.
[159] Chambers, *Popular Rhymes*, p. 380.
[160] Ibid., p. 162.

himself plenty of graves to dig in the year ahead.[161]

---

[161] *Scots Weekly Magazine 1832-33*, p.53.

## 6: *The end of the season*

> "On Christmas night I turned the spit,
> I burned my fingers – I find it yet."

> "Yule's come, and Yule's gane,
> And we hae feasted weel;
> Sae Jock maun to his flail again,
> And Jenny to her wheel."[162]

Twelfth Night and Epiphany were never much celebrated in Scotland after the Reformation:[163] therefore the end of Yuletide on the mainland fell on Handsel

---

[162] Children's rhymes quoted by Chambers, *Popular Rhymes*, pp. 161-62. Chambers notes that the first couplet, a rare use of the word "Christmas", was known across Lowland Scotland; the latter verse, using the more common term Yule and apparently associated with the couplet, was collected in Fife.
[163] There is, for instance, no historical evidence for the wassailing of apple trees in Scotland, an English Twelfth Night custom transferred in some areas to 16th/17th January by the calendar shift: though in the present century it has become increasingly popular.

Monday – the first Monday of January. (After the 1752 calendar shift, Handsel Monday continued to be celebrated on the Julian date, counting the beginning of the year from the twelfth of January rather than the first; by Victorian times the second Monday was often substituted, regardless of whether it fell before or after the twelfth; and as time went on the first Monday seems to have regained its status. By the twentieth century it had almost entirely given place to New Year's Day.) The end of feasting and return to work (before a burn sustained on Yule-Een had time to heal, as in the rhyme above) was lamented but accepted. This was a more mundane end to the season than that decreed in 1456, when King James II ordered that the men of every county should assemble on the first day after the end of Christmas feasting for a "weapon-schawing", parading in arms before the local Crown officers to demonstrate their readiness for war.[164]

A "handsel" was a gift, and Handsel Monday was the season in Scotland for gift-giving, as New Year's Day was once in England: though both seem to have already

---

[164] Taylor, *Pictorial History, Vol. I*, p. 341.

been falling out of use some time before Queen Victoria and Prince Albert popularised the German custom of exchanging presents on Christmas Day. Handsel was expected from one's employers and all their associates,[165] and by schoolmasters from their pupils.[166] This was also the day on which families foregathered, earlier celebrations having been shared rather with neighbours and schoolmates and the wider community.

First-footing, now exclusively a New Year's custom, was sometimes historically associated with Handsel Monday, as were midnight toasts to the year ahead; some celebrators were rebuked for "clipping the wings of the Sabbath" by retiring to bed early on Sunday night so that they could rise early for these festivities. Midnight was particularly boisterous in Newburgh, where the boys of the town would blow horns, light fires, and remove or swap house and street signs. Drinking, singing, and story-telling regularly lasted into the Tuesday, during which time no guests

---

[165] Penny, *Traditions of Perth*, pp. 40-41.
[166] Henderson, *Notes on the folklore of the northern counties*, p. 77.

could be turned away. [167] In Perth, apprentice glovers would turn the parings of leather into tiny purses and sell them for a penny apiece to fund the day's celebrations.[168]

Another Perth custom was hen-and-hesp day, or leg-and-loaf day, a market held the preceding Friday. It owed its names to the practice of farmers' wives bringing chickens and hanks of yarn to sell or exchange for bread and a leg of lamb, to furnish the table for the celebrations on the Monday. It was said that families too poor to afford butcher meat more than once a year would forego it on Yule Day itself to enjoy their Handsel Monday lamb.[169]

In the Shetlands, Handsel Monday was not much celebrated. Instead, the full holiday ended at the New Year, and a sort of half-holiday, dancing and drinking continuing alongside light work, persisted until Twenty-fourth Night – i.e. 17th January, the original date of the famous Up-Helly-Aa.

---

[167] Simpkins, *County Folk-Lore: Fife*, pp. 148-49.
[168] Penny, op. cit., p. 40.
[169] Ibid., p. 142.

"Mak' the maist o' ony chance,
Yule is time to drink and dance.
New'r'mas lucky lines sood bring,
Twenty-fourth night, get the ring.
Gie the lass a kiss, and mind
Time and time are easy tined."[170]

---

[170] Black and Thomas, *County Folk-Lore: Orkney and Shetland*, p. 202.

## Bibliography

*Accounts of the Lord High Treasurer of Scotland* (13v., Edinburgh, 1877 – 1902)

Anderson, William, *Rhymes, Reveries, and Reminiscences* (Aberdeen, 1851)

angusfolklore.blogspot.com

Barrett, Michael, *A calendar of Scottish saints* (Fort Augustus, 1919)

https://www.bbc.co.uk/sounds/series/p02nrtq1

Bede, *De Temporum Ratione*

bequiet.media/scotland-scottish-history-podcast

Black, G. F. (collector), and Thomas, Northcote W. (editor), *County Folk-Lore Vol. III: Examples of Printed Folk-Lore concerning the Orkney and Shetland Islands* (London, 1903)

Burnett, George: see *Exchequer Rolls of Scotland*

Campbell, John Francis, *Popular Tales of the West Highlands* (4v., Paisley and London, 1890; originally published 1859-62)

Carmichael, Alexander, *Carmina Gadelica* (3v., Edinburgh, 1900)

Chambers, Robert, *Popular Rhymes of Scotland*, 3rd edition (Edinburgh and London, 1841)

*The Book of Days: A Miscellany of Popular Antiquities in Connection with the Calendar* (2v., Edinburgh and London, 1864)

Cobbett, William, *Cobbett's parliamentary history of England, from the Norman conquest, in 1066, to the year, 1803* (36v., London, 1810)

Coleman, Keith: see angusfolklore.blogspot.com www.comrie.org

Crockett, Samuel Rutherford, *Raiderland: All about Grey Galloway, its stories, traditions, characters, and humours* (London, 1904)

Cromek, R. H., *Remains of Nithsdale and Galloway Song: with Historical Notices relative to the Manners and Customs of the Peasantry* (London, 1810)

Dalyell, John Graham, *The darker superstitions of Scotland, illustrated from history and practice* (Edinburgh, 1834)

Douglas, Hugh, *The Hogmanay Companion* (2nd edition) (Glasgow, 2000)

*The Exchequer Rolls of Scotland, 1326 – 1600* (23v., Edinburgh, 1878 – 1908)

Fergusson, Robert, *The Works of Robert Fergusson; with a short account of his life, and a concise glossary* (Edinburgh, 1805)

Fergusson, Robert Menzies, *Rambles in the Far North* (London, 1884)
*Folk-lore: A Quarterly Review* (journal, 1890 ff.)
Folklore Podcast, The: see thefolklorepodcast.com
Foster, Henry Clapham, *At Antwerp and the Dardanelles* (London, 1918)
Gaster, Theodor H., *Thespis: Ritual, Myth, and Drama in the Ancient Near East* (New York, 1961)
*Glasgow Times*
Gone Medieval: see https://podfollow.com
Guthrie, E. J., *Old Scottish Customs: local and general* (London and Glasgow, 1885)
Henderson, William, *Notes on the folk-lore of the northern counties of England and the borders* (London, 1878)
Jarman, Cat: see https://podfollow.com
Johnstone, Jenny: see https://www.storiesofscotland.com
Law, Robert, *Memorialls, or the Memorable Things that fell out within this Island of Brittain from 1638 to 1684*, ed. Sharpe, Charles Kirkpatrick (Edinburgh, 1818)
Lynn, Elizabeth, *Witch Stories* (London, 1861)

McCormick, Andrew, *The Tinkler-Gypsies of Galloway* (Dumfries, 1906)
MacDonald, Annie: see https://www.storiesofscotland.com
McIlwraith, Euan: see https://www.bbc.co.uk
McNeill, F. Marian, *The Scots Kitchen* (Edinburgh, 1929)
*The New Statistical Account of Scotland* (15v., Edinburgh, 1845)
Norman, Mark: see thefolklorepodcast.com
*Orkneyinga Saga*
orkneyjar.com
Park, Michael: see bequiet.media
pastandpottage.wordpress.com
Penny, George, *Traditions of Perth* (Perth, 1836)
https://podfollow.com/gone-medieval
Rennie, Susan, and Land, Matthew, *The 12 Days o Yule* (Edinburgh, 2015)
Rodger, Jean, *Lang Strang* (Forfar, 1948)
Rogers, Charles, *Social Life in Scotland from Early to Recent Times* (Edinburgh, 1884)
*The Schoolmaster, and Edinburgh Weekly Magazine, Vols. 1-2* (Edinburgh, 1833)
Scotland (podcast): see bequiet.media
Scotland Outdoors: see https://www.bbc.co.uk

*The Scots Weekly Magazine: A Repertory of Literary Entertainment. Original and Selected. November 1832 to April 1833* (Edinburgh, 1833)

Simpkins, John Ewart, *County Folk-Lore Vol. VII: Examples of Printed Folk-lore Concerning Fife with Some Notes on Clackmannan and Kinross-shires* (London, 1914)

Sinclair, John, *The Statistical Account of Scotland 1791-99* (21v., Edinburgh, 1791-99)

Skinner, John, *Amusements of Leisure Hours: or Poetical Pieces, Chiefly in the Scottish Dialect* (Edinburgh, 1809)

https://soundcloud.com/you-better-run-records/sets/tales-from-wyrd-scotland

Stephen, Mark: see https://www.bbc.co.uk

Stewart, Gordon: see https://soundcloud.com

https://www.storiesofscotland.com/podcast

Sutherland, Catriona: see pastandpottage.wordpress.com

Tales from Wyrd Scotland: see https://soundcloud.com

Taylor, Elizabeth, *Braemar Highlands: Their Tales, Traditions and History* (Edinburgh, 1869)

Taylor, James, *The Pictorial History of Scotland, From The Roman Invasion to the*

*Close of the Jacobite Rebellion. A.D. 79 – 1746* (London, 1859)

Temperley, Alan, *Tales of Galloway* (London, 1979)

thefolklorepodcast.com

Thomas, Northcote W.: *see* Black, G. F.

Thomson, George L., *Traditional Scottish Recipes* (Edinburgh, 1976)

Towrie, Sigurd: see orkneyjar.com

Warren, Janet, *A Feast of Scotland* (London, 1990)

Watson, William, *Glimpses o' Auld Lang Syne* (Aberdeen, 1905)

www.ingramcontent.com/pod-product-compliance
Lightning Source LLC
Chambersburg PA
CBHW071307040426
42444CB00009B/1903